Yolanda's

All New

Cranberry Cookbook

Best Wishes –
Yolanda Lodi

Also by Yolanda Lodi

———

Yolanda's Cranberry Country Recipes

Yolanda's Hand-Me-Down Recipes

Yolanda's Blueberry Cookbook

Yolanda's

All New

Cranberry Cookbook

Yolanda Lodi

ROCK VILLAGE
PUBLISHING

Middleborough, Massachusetts

First Printing

ISBN 978-1-934400-10-4

Rock Village Publishing
41 Walnut Street
Middleborough MA 02346

(508) 946-4738

rockvillage@verizon.net

Dedication

To Carolyn Gilmore

In appreciation of her friendship and artistic talents.

Contents

Side Dishes

Entrées

Cakes

Special Occasion Cake

Buckle, Cobbler, & Crisps

Pies & Puddings

Cookies & Sweets

Yolanda's

All New

Cranberry Cookbook

Introduction

A Peek at What's Inside

With one or two exceptions, the recipes in *Yolanda's All New Cranberry Cookbook* are nutritious and easy to prepare. One of my favorites is Berry Berry Crisp, appropriately named in honor of my two top berries, cranberries and blueberries. This creation deserves a special mention because of how it came about. Frequently throughout the process of writing this cookbook I would hear my husband say the word "snack." Knowing of his fondness for both berries and oatmeal (and that he was tired of having plain oatmeal for breakfast) I came up with this recipe. This satisfied his fruit and fiber fix for the day.

Although the above recipe contains blueberries it does not appear in my previous book, *Yolanda's Blueberry Cookbook*, nor does it appear in *Yolanda's Cranberry Country Recipes*, or even, *Yolanda's Hand-Me-Down Recipes*. These are all brand new recipes for those who love collecting my cookbooks and want to whip-up a new cranberry treat or entrée.

"Most of your recipes use ingredients that already sit on my kitchen shelves," is a frequent comment that I hear when asking what my readers like most about my cookbooks. Many of these recipes comply as long as you have fresh or frozen cranberries, or

3

sweetened dried cranberries. As for me, I always have cranberries in my freezer. During harvest season I purchase several pounds of cranberries. When I get home I sort through them, removing twigs, stems, and rotten berries. Then I wash them in cold water and leave them on a clean towel to dry. (Make sure they're completely dry!) Once they're dry I fill freezer bags with these ruby red berries.

When a recipe calls for frozen cranberries, cut in half or chopped, it's best to cut or chop them while they're still frozen. Cut them the night before and place them in the refrigerator to thaw. When you're ready to make the recipe take the cut cranberries out of the refrigerator and place them on a paper towel to dry. Although Cranberry Biscuits, Cranberry Corn Bread, Cape Cod Blueberry Buckle, Cape Cod Corn Muffins, and Annie Eaton Noble's Cranberry Cake are best made with fresh cranberries, thawed previously frozen berries fit the bill just fine. I'm speaking from experience; I ran out of fresh cranberries from my purchased stash and was forced to use frozen berries.

When looking for a birthday cake using cranberries, look no further than Annie Eaton Noble's Cranberry Cake. The finished cake stands high with a luscious pink frosting that's irresistible. Any child (or adult) will look forward to blowing out the candles on this cake.

If you want to surprise someone with a special coffeecake, Red Ribbon Coffeecake will delight your guests. As soon as they take a mouthful they will discover a ribbon of cranberry filling running across their taste buds. What a pleasant surprise!

Speaking of surprises: how about Granny's Freckled Pie? This one I've made several times. The last was for a Christmas celebration dinner to which I invited special friends, Faye and Winston. The combination of cranberries and Granny Smith Apples left my guests wanting more. Next time we get together I plan on baking another favorite, Mile-High Bumbleberry Pie. It's similar, incorporating my other choice berry, blueberry.

Since we're on the subject of pies I need to mention Nana's Nantucket Cranberry Pie, for those who prefer their pies on the sweet side. This pie is sure to please.

Looking for pie for breakfast? Look no further than Cranberry Apple Breakfast Pie. Invite a couple of friends over for breakfast and serve them this pie. It doesn't take long to make and goes great with any specialty coffee.

Inviting friends for a special dinner? Here are a couple of entrées to serve your cranberry-loving friends. For the true vegetarian there's Squash Delights, which uses both cranberries and apples, Wild About Rice, which uses sweetened dried cranberries (for those who prefer a slightly sweeter taste), Cranberry Stuffed Squash, which uses Instant Brown Rice, and Roasted Sweet Potatoes, which may fool some of your guests. It looks like a dessert!

For those who prefer meat with their sweet potatoes, there's Sweet Potato Chicken, a great combination of taste and colors. Other chicken recipes are Spicy Cranberry Chicken, Cranberry Apple Chicken, and Cranberry Stir-Fry.

Turkey lovers can look forward to Quick and Easy Cranberry Turkey Balls and Cranberry Turkey Loaf. The latter makes two loaves, and I must admit, the first time I made this recipe, my husband and I ate one whole loaf between us. It's that good!

On a more healthful side take a look at Carolyn's Rosy Applesauce and A Crock of Cranberries and Apples. Both are by Carolyn Gilmore, who strives to cook nutritious, healthful foods using vegetables she grows in her garden along with local produce. All that's needed is a crock pot and the love to experiment with cranberries, apples, and spices. So get your crock pot and let me know how it all turns out. Who knows, maybe there's another cookbook author out there?

For the seafood connoisseur I came up with Cranberry Honey Baked Salmon. Both my husband and I enjoy salmon so much that I found this one easy to develop. I hope you enjoy it, too.

Another recipe that came easy was Cranberry Cocoa Bites. It uses unsweetened cocoa powder, which according to recent studies contains certain substances that are good for you. Keeping this in mind I definitely had more than my share of "bites."

Oatmeal is another food that provides many health benefits. Besides the Berry Berry Crisp mentioned earlier there are other recipes using at least one cup of rolled oats — Cranberry Oatmeal

Cookies, Cranberry Oatmeal Surprise, and Oatmeal Harvest Crisp. The latter uses one and one-half cups of rolled oats.

You're probably now saying, "Enough about what's good for me. What about some of the other recipes?" Well, there are several cake recipes that I haven't mentioned yet, such as Cranberry Spice Cake, Pineapple Cranberry Upside-Down Cake, Cranberry Nut Cake, Ruby Raisin Cake, and my husband's favorite, Cranberry Carrot Cake. The latter takes awhile to make but is worth it!

If you're looking for something quick with carrots there's Cranberry Carrot Bread. Other breads that are easy to make are Cranberry Banana Bread, Norma's Cranberry Pumpkin Bread, Cranberry Cottage Bread (named for the cottage cheese ingredient), and Cranberry Sunshine Bread. The latter two contain dried apricots, which give both a special flavor.

Sweetened dried cranberries, either plain as a snack or in baked goods, have become quite popular in today's market. Quite a few recipes in this cookbook use sweetened dried cranberries, such as Speckled Hermits, Cranberry Scones, Blushing Betty, and Cranberry Brioche Bread Pudding, a special recipe given to me by Chef Irene O'Gara and the only recipe I have not made yet because it was perfect when I tasted it. And who am I to question Chef O'Gara?

My pudding creation is Crusty Cranberry Pudding. It's for anyone who loves the tartness of cranberries. If you prefer yours on the sweet side, then Sweet and Crusty Cranberry Cobbler will fit the bill. It's a little too sweet for me, so next time I make it I'll decrease the amount of sugar.

Sweetened flaked coconut is used in Cranberry Macaroons and Cranberry Shortcake. The combination of coconut and cranberries adds a special sweetness and texture to each bite.

Speaking of special, how about a Cranberry Walnut Pizza? This is so easy and fun to make that a child (with adult supervision) could create one for a fun dessert.

As you may have gathered from reading this short introduction, I'm having fun in sharing these recipes with you. My goal in writing this book is to encourage those who love to cook to experiment and take the plunge. Try something new that sounds good. Start with fresh ingredients that you're familiar with and then experiment. Write the recipe, or better still, type it up on your computer and print a hard copy. As you're making the recipe make the necessary adjustments and jot them down. You don't want to leave that perfect recipe to memory. Before you know it you will have created your own cookbook to share with family and friends!

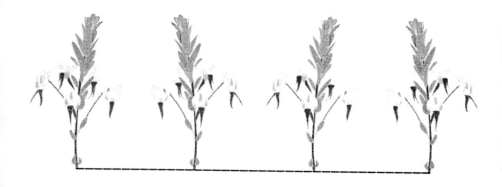

Breakfast & Brunch

Cranberry Brioche Bread Pudding

There's always a treat waiting for folks who attend the annual Donald J. McNamara Scholarship Fund Autumn Craft Fair at Somerset High School. After setting up our book display I sat down to enjoy this bread pudding with a cup of coffee. As soon as I took my first bite I knew I would have to include this wonderful recipe in my next cookbook. At my request, Val McNamara kindly contacted Chef Irene O'Gara and forwarded the recipe to me. A special thanks to both of you.

1 loaf (7 cups) of Brioche Bread (or Challah), crusts removed, diced into one-inch cubes
2 cups sweetened dried cranberries
½ cup fresh orange juice
4 cups half-and-half
4 cups heavy cream
1 vanilla bean, split and scraped
2 cups sugar
12 whole large eggs

Preheat oven to 300 degrees.

Toast bread cubes on a cookie sheet in oven at 300 degrees until dried out and slightly browned.

Remove from oven. Cool completely.

In a small saucepan, plump sweetened dried cranberries in orange juice over low heat, until juice has evaporated. Set aside to cool.

To make custard: Heat creams and vanilla bean over low heat until scalded (just under a simmer). Remove from stove. Let sit for 30 minutes. Then discard vanilla bean.

In a large mixing bowl, whisk sugar and eggs until very well blended.

Slowly, add hot cream to egg and sugar mixture while whisking constantly, so as to not curdle the eggs.

Place toasted bread cubes in a 13- x 9- x 2-inch baking pan. Sprinkle cranberries over the top. Pour custard over the top of the cranberries. Push down floating bread with a spoon. Let sit for 30 minutes.

Place pan inside a larger pan containing one to two inches of water.

Bake uncovered at 300 degrees for one hour or until custard sets. Ready when custard is very puffy and golden brown.

Serve warm.

Makes 12 servings.

Cranberry Banana Bread

⅓ cup butter, melted
¾ cup sugar
2 large eggs
1½ cups all-purpose flour
1 Tbsp. baking powder
½ tsp. salt
2 medium-sized ripe bananas, mashed
1 cup fresh cranberries, cut in half
½ cup chopped walnuts

Preheat oven to 350 degrees.

Grease and flour a 9- x 5- x 3-inch loaf pan.

In a large bowl, with mixer at low speed, cream butter and sugar until light and fluffy. Add one egg at a time, making sure batter continues to be fluffy.

In a separate bowl combine flour, baking powder, and salt. Add dry ingredients to large bowl, stirring with a spoon until smooth.

Fold in bananas, cranberries, and chopped walnuts.

Pour batter into greased and floured loaf pan.

Bake at 350 degrees for 50 to 55 minutes or until toothpick inserted in center comes out clean.

Cool on a wire rack.

Makes 1 loaf.

Cranberry Carrot Bread

2 cups all-purpose flour
1 Tbsp. baking powder
1 tsp. ground cinnamon
½ tsp. ground allspice
½ tsp. salt
2 large eggs
2 cups carrots, grated
⅓ cup extra-virgin olive oil
⅔ cup sugar
¼ cup skim milk
1 tsp. vanilla extract
½ cup sweetened dried cranberries
½ cup chopped walnuts

Preheat oven to 350 degrees.

Grease and flour a 9- x 5- x 3-inch loaf pan.

In a large bowl combine flour, baking powder, cinnamon, allspice, and salt. Mix with a spoon.

In a medium-sized bowl beat eggs with a fork. Add grated carrots, olive oil, sugar, skim milk, and vanilla extract. Stir until combined.

Add carrot mixture to the large bowl. Mix with a spoon until the dry ingredients are moistened.

Fold in sweetened dried cranberries and chopped walnuts.

Pour batter into greased and floured loaf pan.

Bake at 350 degrees for 50 to 55 minutes or until toothpick inserted in center comes out clean.

Cool on a wire rack.

Makes 1 loaf.

Cranberry Corn Bread

2 cups all-purpose flour
1 cup yellow cornmeal
¾ cup sugar
1 Tbsp. baking powder
½ tsp. salt
1 cup cranberries, fresh or frozen (thawed),
    cut in half
2 large eggs
1½ cups skim milk
1 Tbsp. butter, melted

_____

Preheat oven to 400 degrees.

Grease and flour a 13- x 9- x 2-inch baking pan.

In a large bowl sift together flour, cornmeal, sugar, baking powder, and salt. Stir in cranberries.

In a medium-sized bowl whisk eggs. Add milk and melted butter. Whisk until foamy. Add to the large bowl. Mix with a spoon until the dry ingredients are moistened.

Pour batter into greased and floured baking pan.

Bake at 400 degrees for 35 25 minutes or until tooth-pick inserted in center comes out clean.

Cool on a wire rack.

Makes 12 to 15 servings.

Cranberry Cottage Bread

½ cup (1 stick) butter, softened
²/₃ cup dark-brown sugar
2 large eggs
1 cup cottage cheese
3 cups all-purpose flour
3 tsp. baking powder
1 tsp. baking soda
½ tsp. salt
1 cup dried apricots, finely chopped
1 cup sweetened dried cranberries, finely
    chopped

Preheat oven to 350 degrees.

Grease and flour a 9- x 5- x 3-inch loaf pan.

In a large bowl, with mixer at low speed, cream butter and sugar until smooth and fluffy. Add one egg at a time, making sure batter continues to be fluffy.

Stir in cottage cheese until well blended.

In a separate bowl combine flour, baking powder, baking soda, salt, dried apricots and sweetened dried cranberries.

Add to the large bowl. Mix with a spoon until the dry ingredients are moistened. (Batter will be stiff.)

Pour batter into greased and floured loaf pan.

Bake at 350 degrees for 50 to 55 minutes or until toothpick inserted in center comes out clean.

Cool on a wire rack.

Makes 1 loaf.

Cranberry Sunshine Bread

2 cups all-purpose flour
1 cup sugar
1 Tbsp. baking powder
½ tsp. salt
1 cup dried apricots, finely chopped
1 cup fresh cranberries, cut in half
½ cup chopped walnuts
2 large eggs
1 cup skim milk
¼ cup (½ stick) butter, melted
½ tsp. lemon extract

Preheat oven to 350 degrees.

Grease and flour a 9- x 5- x 3-inch loaf pan.

In a large bowl combine flour, sugar, baking powder, and salt. Mix with a spoon. Add apricots, cranberries, and walnuts. Toss gently until fruits are covered.

In a small bowl beat eggs with a fork. Add milk, melted butter, and lemon extract. Stir until combined.

Add to the large bowl. Mix with a spoon until the dry ingredients are moistened.

Pour batter into greased and floured loaf pan.

Bake at 350 degrees for 60 to 65 minutes or until toothpick inserted in center comes out clean.

Cool on a wire rack.

Makes 1 loaf.

Norma's Cranberry Pumpkin Bread

Norma DiCarlo graciously shared this cranberry pumpkin bread recipe with me along with another recipe which I've included later in this cookbook. This is one of my favorite breads for several reasons. The combination of pumpkin and cranberries not only makes for a colorful presentation but also tastes indescribably delicious. Another is that the recipe makes two loaves, one for now and another for later, or to bring to that special someone. This bread freezes extremely well. Take the frozen bread out of the freezer the night before; the next day you'll have cranberry pumpkin bread that tastes like it was made fresh today. Enjoy!

1 can (15 oz.) pumpkin
2 cups sugar
2 large eggs, beaten with a fork
¼ cup extra-virgin olive oil
1 cup applesauce
4 cups all-purpose flour
1 Tbsp. ground cinnamon
1 Tbsp. ground nutmeg
1 Tbsp. baking powder
1 tsp. baking soda
1½ cups fresh cranberries, cut in half
1 cup chopped walnuts

Preheat oven to 350 degrees.

Grease and flour two 9- x 5- x 3-inch loaf pans.

In a large bowl combine pumpkin, sugar, eggs, olive oil, and applesauce. Mix with a spoon.

In another large bowl combine flour, cinnamon, nutmeg, baking powder, and baking soda. Add dry ingredients to pumpkin mixture, stirring with a spoon until combined.

Fold in cranberries and chopped walnuts.

Pour batter into greased and floured loaf pans.

Bake at 350 degrees for 60 to 65 minutes or until toothpick inserted in center comes out clean.

Cool on a wire rack.

Makes 2 loaves.

Cape Cod Corn Muffins

1 cup all-purpose flour
1 cup yellow cornmeal
¾ cup sugar
1½ Tbsp. baking powder
1 large egg
¾ cup skim milk
⅓ cup extra-virgin olive oil
1 cup cranberries, fresh or frozen (thawed),
      cut in half

Preheat oven to 425 degrees.

Grease twelve-2½-inch-muffin-cup pan well with butter.

In a large bowl combine flour, cornmeal, sugar, and baking powder.

In a medium-sized bowl whisk egg. Add milk and olive oil. Whisk until foamy.

Add to the large bowl. Stir with a spoon until the dry ingredients are moistened.

Fold in cranberries.

Spoon batter into muffin pan.

Bake at 425 degrees for 15 to 20 minutes or until toothpick inserted in center comes out clean.

Makes 12 muffins.

Cranberry Biscuits

2 cups all-purpose flour
¾ cup sugar
2 tsp. baking powder
½ tsp. salt
1 large egg
½ cup orange juice with pulp
⅓ cup extra-virgin olive oil
1 cup cranberries, fresh or frozen (thawed),
    cut in half
2 Tbsp. chopped walnuts

Preheat oven to 400 degrees.

Grease twelve-2½-inch-muffin-cup pan well with butter.

In a large bowl combine flour, sugar, baking powder, and salt. Mix with a spoon.

In a medium-sized bowl whisk egg. Then add orange juice and olive oil. Whisk until foamy.

Add to the large bowl. Mix with a spoon until the dry ingredients are moistened.

Fold in cranberries.

Spoon batter into muffin pan. Sprinkle chopped walnuts on top.

Bake at 400 degrees for 20 minutes or until toothpick inserted in center comes out clean.

Makes 12 muffins.

Cranberry Scones

2½ cups all-purpose flour
½ cup sugar
2 tsp. baking powder
1 tsp. baking soda
½ tsp. salt
¼ cup (½ stick) chilled butter, cut into small
     pieces
¼ cup sweetened dried cranberries, finely
     chopped
1 large egg
1 cup vanilla yogurt

Glaze
½ cup confectioners' sugar
1 Tbsp. orange juice

Preheat oven to 425 degrees.

Grease a baking sheet.

In a large bowl combine flour, sugar, baking powder, baking soda, and salt. Using a pastry cutter, cut in butter until mixture forms crumbs. Stir in sweetened dried cranberries.

In a medium-sized bowl whisk egg and yogurt until smooth. Add to large bowl. Mix with a wooden spoon until the dry ingredients are moistened.

Place dough on a lightly floured board and knead gently to form a ball. Divide the dough into two equal balls. Pat each ball into a circle, about six inches in diameter and one-inch thick. Then cut the dough into 6 equal wedges.

Place wedges 2 inches apart onto greased baking sheet.

Bake at 425 degrees for 10 to 13 minutes or until golden brown.

Glaze
In a small bowl mix the glaze ingredients. Let stand while scones are baking.

Remove scones from oven.

Spread glaze on scones while still warm.

Makes 12 scones.

Cranberry Apple Breakfast Pie

3 large eggs
½ cup all-purpose flour
½ cup skim milk
2 Tbsp. (¼ stick) butter
1 large Granny Smith apple, peeled, cored,
    and thinly sliced
½ cup fresh or frozen cranberries, cut in half
1 Tbsp. sugar
1 tsp. ground cinnamon

    Confectioners' sugar
      (to sprinkle over top after baking)

Preheat oven to 450 degrees.

Generously butter the bottom and sides of a 9-inch glass pie plate.

In a medium-sized bowl whisk eggs until foamy. Gradually add flour, whisking after each addition to avoid lumps. Slowly add milk and continue to whisk until batter is smooth. Set aside.

In a medium saucepan melt butter over medium heat. Add apples, cranberries, sugar, and cinnamon. Cook and stir over medium-high heat until apples are tender and cranberries pop.

Spread apple and cranberry mixture evenly on bottom of the pie plate.

Pour batter over the apple and cranberry mixture.

Bake at 450 degrees for 15 to 18 minutes or until golden brown.

Serve immediately with a generous sprinkle of confectioners' sugar.

Make 4 servings.

"Bottoms Up" Cranberry Squares

2½ cups fresh cranberries
½ cup dark-brown sugar, firmly packed
½ cup chopped walnuts
2 large eggs
1 cup granulated sugar
1 cup all-purpose flour
2/3 cup butter, melted

Preheat oven to 325 degrees.

Generously butter a 13- x 9- x 2-inch baking pan. Then place cranberries evenly on bottom of pan.

Sprinkle brown sugar and chopped walnuts over the cranberries. Set aside.

In a large bowl beat eggs until foamy. Gradually add granulated sugar, beating after each addition, until mixture is thick and light.

Add flour and melted butter. Beat until well blended.

Using a spatula carefully spread batter evenly over the cranberry mixture that lines the bottom of the pan.

Bake at 325 degrees for 40 to 45 minutes or until top is golden brown. Test by inserting toothpick in center. Ready when pick comes out clean.

Cool in pan on a wire rack for 5 minutes before cutting and inverting squares onto dessert plate.

Serve with whipped cream or ice cream.

Makes 12 squares.

Cranberry Nutmeg Squares

4 cups fresh cranberries, cut in half
2 cups sugar
½ cup extra-virgin olive oil
2 large eggs, beaten with a fork
¼ cup orange juice with pulp
1 tsp. vanilla extract
2 cups all-purpose flour
1 tsp. baking soda
1 tsp. ground nutmeg
1 cup chopped walnuts

Preheat oven to 350 degrees.

Grease a 13- x 9- x 2-inch baking pan.

In a large bowl combine cranberries, sugar, olive oil, eggs, orange juice, and vanilla extract. Stir well until cranberries are covered.

In a separate bowl combine flour, baking soda, nutmeg, and chopped walnuts.

Add dry ingredients to large bowl, stirring with a spoon until the dry ingredients are moistened.

Pour batter into greased pan. Spread evenly into the corners.

Bake at 350 degrees for 40 to 45 minutes until top is golden brown.

Cool completely on a wire rack before cutting.

Makes 24 squares.

Red Ribbon Coffeecake

Filling
2 cups cranberries, fresh or frozen, cut in half
¾ cup sugar
½ cup water

Batter
2 cups all-purpose flour
¾ cup sugar
½ Tbsp. baking powder
½ cup (1 stick) chilled butter, cut into small
        pieces
1 large egg
¾ cup skim milk
1 tsp. vanilla extract

Topping
2 Tbsp. sugar
2 Tbsp. all-purpose flour
1 Tbsp. chilled butter, cut into small pieces

Ground cinnamon (to sprinkle over top)

Sugar (to sprinkle over top)

Preheat oven to 350 degrees.

Grease and flour a 9-inch square baking pan.

Filling
Place all filling ingredients in a small saucepan.

On high heat stir to boiling. Reduce heat to medium. Continue to stir and cook until cranberries pop and mixture has the consistency of jam (*about 5 minutes*).

Remove from heat. Cool completely.

Batter
In a large bowl combine flour, sugar, and baking powder. Using a pastry cutter, cut in butter until mixture forms crumbs.

In a medium-sized bowl whisk egg. Add milk and vanilla extract. Whisk until foamy. Add to the large bowl. Mix with a spoon until the dry ingredients are moistened.

Pour **half** the batter into greased and floured pan. Set aside.

Beat cranberry filling until smooth.

Spread filling over batter in pan. Using a spatula carefully spread the remaining batter over the filling. (Try not to disturb the cranberry filling.)

Topping

In a small bowl mix sugar and flour. Using a pastry cutter cut in butter until mixture forms crumbs.

Sprinkle over batter. Then sprinkle cinnamon and sugar.

Bake at 350 degrees for 30 minutes or until toothpick inserted in center comes out clean.

Makes 9 servings.

Side Dishes

Carolyn's Rosy Applesauce

6 medium baking apples, peeled, cored, and
  chopped
1 cup cranberries, fresh or frozen

Ground cinnamon
  (to sprinkle over top after baking)

Preheat oven to 350 degrees.

Fill a 3-quart round (4-inch deep) glass oven-proof baking dish with chopped apples.

Finish by scattering cranberries over the top of the apples.

Cover dish with aluminum foil. (Carolyn uses a ceramic baking dish with a glass cover.)

Bake at 350 degrees for 50 to 60 minutes or until apples start coming apart and cranberries bubble.

Remove from oven.

Stir with wooden spoon.

Sprinkle with cinnamon.

Cool slightly.

 Serve warm.

Makes about 4 cups.

A Crock of Cranberries and Apples

Carolyn Gilmore cooks nutritious, healthy foods using local produce while always trying to incorporate cranberries into a recipe. The recipe below came as a result of her original recipe "Rosy Applesauce" found on the previous page. For crock pot lovers who love the smell of apples cooking, love to experiment, and need no specific amounts in assembling a recipe, this recipe is for you.

> Crock Pot
> Baking apples, peeled, cored, and chopped into
> chunks
> Cranberries, fresh or frozen
> Sugar to taste
> Cinnamon to taste

Carolyn's easy instructions:
Just fill the crock pot to the top with apple chunks, sprinkle a handful or two of cranberries, and cook 4 hours on high (maybe all day on low). When it cooks down, stir with a wooden spoon until fully blended. Then add sugar and cinnamon to taste.

Cranberry Stuffed Squash

2 small acorn squashes, cut in half lengthwise
and seeds removed

Stuffing
2 Tbsp. extra-virgin olive oil
1 small red onion, minced
2 garlic cloves, minced
2 tsp. Old Bay® Seasoning
1 cup Instant Brown Rice
1¾ cups water
½ cup sweetened dried cranberries
½ cup chopped walnuts

Preheat oven to 350 degrees.

Coat a glass oven-proof baking dish with olive oil.

Place squash cut-side down in baking dish and cover tightly with aluminum foil.

Bake at 350 degrees for 55 to 60 minutes or until squash is tender.

Stuffing

In a large saucepan heat olive oil. Add onion, garlic cloves, and Old Bay® Seasoning. Sauté until soft, but not browned (*about 3 to 5 minutes*).

Stir in rice and water. Bring to a boil.

Reduce heat to low and cover pan. Cook without stirring for 25 minutes or until tender and water is absorbed.

Remove from stovetop.

Stir in sweetened dried cranberries and chopped walnuts.

Divide the stuffing into 4 equal portions. Using an ice cream scoop mound the center of the cooked squash halves with the mixture.

Makes 4 servings.

43

Squash Delights

3 small acorn squashes, cut in half lengthwise
    and seeds removed

Filling
1 cup cranberries, fresh or frozen, cut in half
1 medium apple, peeled, cored, and chopped
¼ cup dark-brown sugar, firmly packed
2 Tbsp. butter, melted
¼ cup chopped walnuts

Preheat oven to 350 degrees.

Coat a glass oven-proof baking dish with olive oil.

Place squash cut-side down in baking dish.

Bake at 350 degrees for 35 minutes.

Remove from oven. Set aside to cool slightly.

Filling

In a medium-sized bowl combine cranberries, chopped apple, brown sugar, and butter. Toss gently until fruits are covered.

Turn cut-side up and fill squash with fruit mixture. Sprinkle chopped walnuts on top.

Cover with aluminum foil.

Bake for an **additional** 30 to 35 minutes or until squash is tender.

Cool slightly before serving.

Makes 6 servings.

Roasted Sweet Potatoes

3 medium sweet potatoes, peeled and cubed
2 Granny Smith apples, peeled, cored, and
    cubed
2 Tbsp. extra-virgin olive oil
1 cup cranberries, fresh of frozen
1 Tbsp. honey

Topping
¼ cup sweetened flaked coconut
1 Tbsp. dark-brown sugar, firmly packed
1 Tbsp. chopped walnuts
1 tsp. ground ginger
1 tsp. ground cinnamon
⅛ tsp. salt

Preheat oven to 450 degrees.

Lightly grease a 13- x 9- x 2-inch baking pan.

In a large bowl combine sweet potatoes, apples, and olive oil. Toss gently until potatoes and apples absorb the olive oil. Spread evenly on bottom of baking pan. Then sprinkle cranberries over the top and drizzle honey. Cover with aluminum foil.

Bake at 450 degrees for the **first** 10 minutes.

Lower oven temperature to 350 degrees. Bake an **additional** 45 to 50 minutes or until potatoes are tender.

While the sweet potatoes and apples are roasting prepare topping:
In a small bowl combine all ingredients. Set aside until ready to use.

Remove pan from oven and sprinkle topping over casserole.

Return pan to oven and bake (uncovered) an **additional** 5 minutes.

Makes 6 servings.

Wild About Rice

2 Tbsp. extra-virgin olive oil
2 cups celery, chopped
1 cup red onion, chopped
1 can (14 oz.) vegetable broth
1 cup water
2/3 cup wild rice, rinsed and drained
1/3 cup sweetened dried cranberries
1/4 cup walnuts, finely diced

In a large saucepan heat olive oil. Add celery and onions. Sauté until soft, but not browned. Add broth and water. Bring to a full boil.

Stir in rice. Reduce heat to low. Cover and simmer for about 60 minutes or until rice is tender and most of the liquid is absorbed.

Stir in sweetened dried cranberries and finely diced walnuts.

Continue to cook uncovered until all liquid is absorbed.

Fluff with a fork and serve.

Makes 6 to 8 servings.

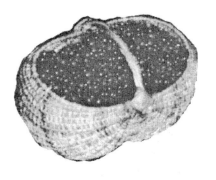

Entrées

Cranberry Apple Chicken

2 lbs. chicken breasts, boneless and skinless, cut in half and flattened
¼ cup bread crumbs

Sauce
½ cup water
¼ cup sugar
1 cup fresh or frozen cranberries
1 medium baking apple, peeled, cored, and chopped

Preheat oven to 400 degrees.

Butter an oven-proof glass dish large enough to contain the chicken breasts.

In a small saucepan combine water and sugar, stirring until sugar dissolves. Bring to a full boil. Reduce heat to low and simmer for 5 minutes.

Add cranberries and chopped apple. Cook over medium-high heat, stirring constantly, until cranberries split and mixture begins to boil. Continue to boil and stir for approximately one minute.

Remove from stove and set aside.

Coat both sides of the chicken pieces with bread crumbs. Place them in buttered dish.

Pour sauce over chicken. Cover with aluminum foil.

Bake at 400 degrees for 30 minutes.

Serve over rice.

Makes 4 servings.

Spicy Cranberry Chicken

2 lbs. chicken breasts, boneless and skinless,
    cut in half and flattened
¼ cup bread crumbs

Sauce
½ cup dark-brown sugar, firmly packed
½ cup water
½ Tbsp. Port wine
¼ tsp. ground cinnamon
⅛ tsp. ground allspice
⅛ tsp. ground cloves
⅛ tsp. salt
1 cup fresh or frozen cranberries

Preheat oven to 400 degrees.

Butter an oven-proof glass dish large enough to contain the chicken breasts.

In a small saucepan mix brown sugar, water, Port wine, spices, and salt. Bring to a slight boil. Reduce heat to medium.

Add cranberries. Cook over medium heat, stirring constantly, until cranberries split and mixture thickens.

Remove from stove and set aside.

Coat both sides of the chicken pieces with bread crumbs. Place them in buttered dish.

Pour sauce over chicken. Cover with aluminum foil.

Bake at 400 degrees for 30 minutes.

Serve over rice.

Makes 4 servings.

Sweet Potato Chicken

2 medium sweet potatoes, peeled and thinly
     sliced
2 lbs. chicken breasts, boneless and skinless,
     cut in half

Sauce
2 cups cranberries, fresh or frozen
½ cup sugar
¼ cup water
¼ cup extra-virgin olive oil
½ tsp. ground ginger
¼ tsp. salt
¼ tsp. ground black pepper

Preheat oven to 400 degrees.

Evenly place sweet potato slices in a 13- x 9- x 2-inch baking pan. Then place chicken on top. Set aside.

Sauce
In a small saucepan combine cranberries, sugar, and water. On high heat stir to boiling.

Reduce heat to medium. Continue to stir and cook until cranberries pop and mixture has the consistency of jam (*about 3 minutes*).

Remove from stove. Add olive oil, ginger, salt, and black pepper. Whisk until combined.

Pour sauce evenly over chicken.

Cover with aluminum foil and bake for 40 minutes.

Makes 4 servings.

Cranberry Stir-Fry

1 lb. turkey breast cutlets, rinsed and dried,
   cut against grain into ⅛-inch-thick strips
1 package (8 oz.) sugar snap peas, cooked
   according to package directions
2 Tbsp. extra-virgin olive oil
¼ cup sweetened dried cranberries

Sauce
2 Tbsp. soy sauce
1 Tbsp. red wine
½ Tbsp. cornstarch
3 Tbsp. water
½ tsp. ground black pepper

In a small bowl mix soy sauce with red wine. Stir in cornstarch, water, and black pepper. Set aside.

In a large skillet heat olive oil over high heat. When oil starts to smoke add cutlet strips and sauté until cooked, about one minute.

Add cooked sugar snap peas to skillet.

Reduce heat to medium.

Stir sauce until combined and add to skillet. Continue to cook over medium heat, stirring constantly, until sauce begins to boil.

Add sweetened dried cranberries. Continue to boil and stir for approximately one minute or until sauce thickens and turns translucent.

Serve over rice.

Makes 4 servings.

Cranberry Turkey Loaf

There's no reason to buy a "Hungry Man" dinner when you can make this recipe. Preparation time is the same so make two loaves — eat one tonight, freeze the other for another night, if there's any left! This moist loaf can be served with mashed potatoes and your favorite vegetable. Every bite tastes better than the first. Don't be surprised if all of a sudden the whole loaf disappears. That's what happened to us. My husband and I devoured one whole loaf between the two of us. That's how many servings? I'll let you decide. One loaf should feed a family of four very nicely. If not, you do have that second loaf!

Loaf
2 large eggs, beaten with a fork
¼ cup skim milk
½ cup catsup
1 cup jellied cranberry sauce
1 cup onion, chopped
2 cloves garlic, minced
1 cup bread crumbs
¼ tsp. ground black pepper
2½ lbs. ground turkey (93% lean)

Sauce
½ cup catsup
1 cup jellied cranberry sauce
1 Tbsp. lemon juice

Preheat oven to 350 degrees.

Loaf
In a large bowl combine all loaf ingredients **except** ground turkey. Mix well.

Crumble turkey over mixture. Mix thoroughly. (I use my hands.)

Divide turkey loaf mixture in half.

Spread each half in 2 ungreased 9- x 5- x 3-inch loaf pans. Set aside.

Sauce
In a small bowl stir sauce ingredients until smooth.

Pour sauce over top of each loaf.

Bake uncovered for 45 to 55 minutes.

Remove from oven. Allow loaf to rest for 10 minutes before slicing.

Makes 8 to 10 servings.

Quick and Easy
Cranberry Turkey Balls

1 lb. ground turkey (lean)
½ cup bread crumbs
2 large egg whites

Sauce
1 cup jellied cranberry sauce
1 can (8 oz.) tomato sauce
½ cup water

Preheat oven to 350 degrees.

In a large bowl combine ground turkey, bread crumbs, and egg whites. Shape small amounts into one-inch balls and arrange in large baking dish. Cover with aluminum foil.

Bake at 350 degrees for 20 minutes.

While the turkey balls are baking prepare sauce:
In a medium-sized bowl whisk sauce ingredients until smooth. Set aside until ready to use.

Remove pan from oven. Spoon sauce over turkey balls.

Return baking dish to oven and bake (uncovered) an **additional** 30 minutes.

Serve with your favorite pasta.

Makes about 3 dozen turkey balls.

Cranberry Honey Baked Salmon

1-1½ lbs salmon fillets
¼ cup sweetened dried cranberries
1 Tbsp. honey
1 Tbsp. lemon juice (squeezed from a fresh
    lemon)
½ Tbsp. extra-virgin olive oil
⅛ tsp. ground black pepper

Coat an oven-proof glass dish large enough to contain the salmon fillets with olive oil. Place the salmon fillets skin-side down.

In a small bowl combine sweetened dried cranberries, honey, lemon juice, olive oil, and black pepper. Spoon sauce over salmon fillets. Cover with aluminum foil and refrigerate for 30 minutes.

30 minutes later:
Preheat oven to 450 degrees.

Remove salmon from refrigerator. Let stand at room temperature for 15 minutes.

Bake at 450 degrees for 15 to 20 minutes or until salmon flakes easily with a fork.

Makes 2 to 3 servings.

Cakes

Cranberry Nut Cake

½ cup (1 stick) butter, softened
1½ cups dark-brown sugar
1 large egg
2½ cups all-purpose flour
1 tsp. baking soda
½ cup skim milk
1 tsp. vanilla extract
2 cups fresh cranberries, cut in half
1 cup chopped walnuts

Preheat oven to 350 degrees.

Grease a 13- x 9- x 2-inch baking pan.

In a large bowl, with mixer at low speed, cream butter and brown sugar until smooth and fluffy. Add egg, making sure batter continues to be fluffy.

In a separate bowl combine flour and baking soda. Set aside.

Pour milk into a measuring cup. Stir in vanilla extract.

With mixer at medium speed, add dry ingredients to large bowl, alternately with liquid, until well blended. Fold in cranberries and chopped walnuts.

Pour batter into greased pan. Spread evenly into the corners.

Bake at 350 degrees for 30 minutes until top is golden brown. Test by inserting toothpick in center. Ready when pick comes out clean.

Cool completely on a wire rack before cutting.

Makes 12 servings.

Cranberry Spice Cake

½ cup (1 stick) butter, softened
1½ cups sugar
1½ cups applesauce
2¼ cups all-purpose flour
2 tsp. baking soda
1 tsp. salt
1 tsp. ground cinnamon
¼ tsp. ground cloves
1 cup sweetened dried cranberries

Glaze
1 cup confectioners' sugar
1½ Tbsp. orange juice

Preheat oven to 350 degrees.

Generously grease a 13- x 9- x 2-inch baking pan.

In a large bowl, with mixer at low speed, cream butter and sugar until light and fluffy. Stir in applesauce.

In a separate bowl sift together flour, baking soda, salt, cinnamon, and cloves.

Add dry ingredients to large bowl, stirring with a spoon until the dry ingredients are moistened.

Fold in sweetened dried cranberries.

Pour batter into greased pan. Using a spatula spread batter evenly into the corners.

Bake at 350 degrees for 30 minutes or until toothpick inserted in center comes out clean.

Glaze
Measure confectioners' sugar in a large measuring cup. Add orange juice. Mix well with a spoon. Let stand while cake is baking.

Remove cake from oven.

Spread glaze over warm cake.

Serve warm or cold.

Makes 12 servings.

Cranberry Shortcake

2 cups cranberries, fresh or frozen
¾ cup sugar
1 cup water
½ cup orange juice
2/3 cup all-purpose flour
¼ cup sugar
1 tsp. baking powder
⅛ tsp. salt
¼ cup sweetened flaked coconut
2 large egg yolks
2 Tbsp. skim milk
2 Tbsp. butter, melted

In a 3-quart pan combine cranberries, sugar, water, and orange juice. On medium heat bring to a continuous *slow* boil. While waiting, prepare dough.

In a large bowl sift together all-purpose flour, sugar, baking powder, and salt. Stir in coconut.

In a medium-sized bowl whisk egg yolks, milk, and melted butter. Stir into flour mixture. Blend well by hand until dough forms a ball.

Bring cranberry mixture to a full boil, stirring occasionally, until most berries pop.

Divide dough into four equal balls and drop (evenly spaced) on top of the boiling mixture.

Lower heat. Cover and simmer for about 20 minutes.

Spoon into dessert bowls.

Serve warm with whipped cream.

Makes 4 servings.

Pineapple Cranberry
Upside-Down Cake

Batter
½ cup (1 stick) butter, softened
½ cup granulated sugar
1 large egg
1½ cups all-purpose flour
1½ tsp. baking powder
¼ tsp. salt
½ cup skim milk

Topping
3 Tbsp. butter
¾ cup dark-brown sugar, packed
8 pineapple slices, well drained
3 Tbsp. sweetened dried cranberries

Preheat oven to 375 degrees.

Batter
In a large bowl, with mixer at low speed, cream butter and sugar until smooth and fluffy. Add egg, making sure batter continues to be fluffy.

In a separate bowl sift together flour, baking powder, and salt.

With mixer at medium speed, add dry, sifted ingredients to large bowl, alternately with skim milk, until well blended. Set aside.

To assemble the Upside-Down Cake:
Place butter in a 9-inch square baking pan. Melt butter in oven. Remove from oven. Tilt to coat sides.

Sprinkle brown sugar evenly over melted butter. Arrange pineapple slices and fill centers with sweetened dried cranberries.

Using a spatula carefully spread batter evenly over the topping. (Try not to disturb the pineapple and the sweetened dried cranberries.)

Bake at 375 degrees for about 35 minutes or until toothpick inserted in center comes out clean.

Cool in pan on a wire rack for 5 minutes before inverting cake onto serving plate.

Serve warm with whipped cream or your favorite ice cream.

Makes 9 servings.

Ruby Raisin Cake

Topping
¼ cup (½ stick) butter
½ cup dark-brown sugar, firmly packed
1½ cups cranberries, fresh or frozen (thawed)
½ cup golden raisins, plumped

Batter
1¼ cups all-purpose flour
1¼ tsp. baking powder
¼ tsp. salt
3 large eggs
¾ cup granulated sugar
½ cup water
½ tsp. lemon extract

Preheat oven to 350 degrees.

Topping
Place butter in a 9-inch square baking pan. Melt butter in oven. Remove from oven. Tilt to coat sides.

Sprinkle brown sugar evenly over melted butter. Then place cranberries evenly in one layer. Finish with raisins.

Batter
In a medium-sized bowl combine flour, baking powder, and salt. Stir with a spoon. Set aside.

In a large bowl beat eggs until foamy. Gradually add sugar, beating after each addition, until mixture is thick and light. Add water and lemon extract. Beat until well blended.

Fold in flour mixture. Mix with a spoon until the dry ingredients are moistened.

Pour batter over cranberries and raisins.

Bake at 350 degrees for 30 to 35 minutes until top is golden brown. Test by inserting toothpick in center. Ready when pick comes out clean.

Cool in pan on a wire rack for 5 minutes before inverting cake onto serving plate.

Makes 9 servings.

Cranberry Carrot Cake

4 cups carrots, grated
2 cups sugar
1 cup (2 sticks) butter, cut into one-inch pieces
1½ cups undrained crushed pineapple, packed
      in its own juice
3 cups all-purpose flour
2 tsp. baking soda
½ tsp. baking powder
1 Tbsp. ground cinnamon
2 tsp. ground cloves
1 tsp. ground allspice
1 tsp. ground nutmeg
½ tsp. salt
1 cup sweetened dried cranberries
2 large eggs

Preheat oven to 350 degrees.

Grease and flour a 10-inch tube pan.

In a medium saucepan combine carrots, sugar, butter, and pineapple with juice. Cook and stir occasionally over medium-low heat until mixture comes to a boil. Continue to stir for an additional 5 minutes. (Mixture will resemble applesauce.)

Remove from heat. Set aside to cool completely.

In a large bowl combine flour, baking soda, baking powder, cinnamon, cloves, allspice, nutmeg, salt, and sweetened dried cranberries.

In a very large bowl beat eggs until smooth and creamy. Add carrot mixture and stir until combined. Then add flour mixture, stirring with a spoon until the dry ingredients are moistened.

Pour batter into greased and floured pan.

Bake at 350 degrees for 45 to 50 minutes or until toothpick inserted in center comes out clean.

Cool cake for 10 minutes before removing from pan. Frost cake with the following recipe.

Cream Cheese Frosting

1 package (8 oz.) cream cheese, softened
½ cup (1 stick) butter, melted
1 tsp. vanilla extract
2 cups confectioners' sugar
½ cup chopped walnuts
¼ cup sweetened dried cranberries

In a large bowl beat cream cheese, melted butter, and vanilla extract until smooth and fluffy.

Gradually add confectioners' sugar, beating after each addition, until smooth and fluffy.

Stir in chopped walnuts and sweetened dried cranberries.

Makes 12 servings.

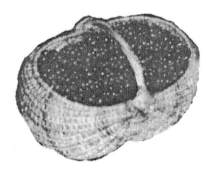

Special Occasion Cake

Annie Eaton Noble's Cranberry Cake

Looking for a special birthday cake, especially for someone who loves cranberries? Look no further than Annie Eaton Noble's Cranberry Cake. This recipe was given to Marilyn Thayer, children's librarian at the Middleborough Public Library, by her friend and mentor Annie Eaton Noble, who lives in Dennisport, Massachusetts, where she breeds cocker spaniels. The two friends not only share their love for cocker spaniels but also enjoy exchanging recipes.

The day I made this recipe I brought a portion of the cake to Marilyn for her taste approval and to share with her colleagues and friends. I mentioned that I used Crisco®, not knowing what type of shortening Annie used. Just before I completed this cookbook Marilyn informed me that Annie uses margarine or whatever other shortening was available during time of war. She's in her eighties and has been baking for many years.

1 cup shortening
1½ cups sugar
4 large eggs
3 cups all-purpose flour
2½ tsp. baking powder
½ tsp. salt
⅔ cup milk
2 cups cranberries, fresh or frozen (thawed), chopped
1 cup pecans, chopped

Preheat oven to 350 degrees.

Grease and flour a 10-inch tube pan.

In a large bowl cream shortening and sugar thoroughly. Add eggs, one at a time, beating well after each addition.

Sift together flour, baking powder, and salt.

Add sifted, dry ingredients to creamed mixture, alternately with milk, blending after each addition.

Fold in cranberries and pecans.

Spread in greased and floured 10-inch tube pan.

Bake at 350 degrees for 1 hour and 20 minutes.

Cool cake before removing from pan. Frost cake with the following recipe, or if desired, sprinkle cake with confectioners' sugar.

Cranberry Frosting

½ cup cranberries, fresh or frozen
¼ cup water
1 Tbsp. lemon juice
¼ cup (½ stick) butter, softened
4 cups confectioners' sugar, sifted

In a small saucepan combine cranberries and water. Cook, stirring occasionally, until berries pop (*about 5 minutes*).

Remove from stove and cool.

Blend in lemon juice.

In a large bowl cream butter.

Add confectioners' sugar, alternately with cranberry mixture, blending after each addition. Add only enough sugar to make a spreading consistency.

Makes 12 servings.

Buckle, Cobbler & Crisps

Cape Cod Blueberry Buckle

¼ cup (½ stick) butter, softened
½ cup sugar
1 large egg
2 cups all-purpose flour
2 tsp. baking powder
½ tsp. salt
¾ cup skim milk
1 cup blueberries, fresh or frozen (thawed)
1 cup cranberries, fresh or frozen (thawed),
    cut in half

Topping
¼ cup (½ stick) butter, softened
½ cup sugar
⅓ cup all-purpose flour
1 tsp. ground cinnamon
¼ cup chopped walnuts

Preheat oven to 350 degrees.

Grease a 9-inch square baking pan.

In a large bowl, with mixer at low speed, cream butter and sugar until light and fluffy. Add egg, making sure batter continues to be fluffy.

In a separate bowl sift together flour, baking powder, and salt.

With mixer at medium speed, add dry ingredients to large bowl, alternately with skim milk, until well blended.

Fold in blueberries and cranberries.

Pour batter into greased pan. Spread evenly into corners. Set aside.

In a medium-sized bowl stir topping ingredients with a fork until crumbly. Sprinkle over top of batter.

Bake at 350 degrees for 45 to 50 minutes or until toothpick inserted in center comes out clean.

Serve warm.

Makes 9 servings.

Sweet and Crusty
Cranberry Cobbler

Cranberry Mixture
2 cups fresh cranberries
¼ cup dark-brown sugar
½ cup chopped walnuts

Batter
2 large eggs
1 cup granulated sugar
1 tsp. vanilla extract
1 cup all-purpose flour
¼ cup (½ stick) butter, melted

Preheat oven to 350 degrees.

Generously butter a 9-inch glass pie plate.

Cranberry Mixture
In a large bowl combine cranberries, brown sugar, and chopped walnuts. Spread mixture evenly over bottom of pie plate. Set aside.

Batter
In a medium-sized bowl beat eggs, sugar, and vanilla extract. Add flour and melted butter. Beat until batter is smooth and fluffy.

Spoon batter evenly over cranberry mixture.

Bake at 350 degrees for 40 minutes or until golden brown.

Cool slightly on a wire rack.

Serve warm with whipped cream or ice cream.

Makes 8 servings.

Berry Berry Crisp

2 cups cranberries, fresh or frozen, cut in half
2 cups blueberries, fresh or frozen
½ cup granulated sugar

Topping
1 cup rolled oats
½ cup all-purpose flour
½ cup dark-brown sugar
⅓ cup chilled butter, cut into small pieces

Preheat oven to 375 degrees.

Butter the bottom and sides of a 9-inch square pan.

In a large bowl combine cranberries, blueberries, and sugar. Toss until berries are covered with sugar.

Line bottom of greased pan with berry mixture. Set aside.

Topping
In a large bowl whisk oats, flour, and brown sugar. Using a pastry cutter, cut in butter until mixture forms crumbs.

Sprinkle topping over berries.

Bake at 375 degrees for 30 to 35 minutes until top is golden brown and juice from the berries bubbles through.

Cool slightly on a wire rack.

Serve warm.

Makes 6 servings.

Oatmeal Harvest Crisp

Apple / Cranberry Mixture
3 medium baking apples, peeled, cored, and
      chopped
2 cups fresh or frozen cranberries
½ cup granulated sugar

Topping
½ cup (1 stick) butter, melted
1½ cups rolled oats
½ cup dark-brown sugar
⅓ cup all-purpose flour
¼ cup chopped walnuts

Preheat oven to 350 degrees.

Butter the bottom and sides of a 13- x 9- x 2-inch glass oven-proof baking dish.

Apple / Cranberry Mixture
In a large bowl combine apples, cranberries, and sugar. Toss until fruits are covered with sugar. Spread evenly over bottom of baking dish. Set aside.

Topping
In a medium-sized bowl stir topping ingredients until combined. Sprinkle evenly over fruits.

Bake at 350 degrees for 35 to 40 minutes or until fruit is soft and juice from the fruits bubbles.

Transfer to cooling wire rack. Cool slightly.

Serve warm.

Makes 12 servings.

Cranberry Oatmeal Surprise

Filling
2 cups cranberries, fresh or frozen, cut in half
½ cup golden raisins
¾ cup granulated sugar
1 Tbsp. cornstarch
⅛ tsp. salt
½ cup water
1 tsp. vanilla extract

Oatmeal Mixture
1 cup rolled oats
½ cup dark-brown sugar
½ cup all-purpose flour
⅓ cup chilled butter, cut into small pieces

Preheat oven to 350 degrees.

Butter the bottom and sides of an 8-inch square pan.

In a medium saucepan combine cranberries, raisins, sugar, cornstarch, and salt. Stir in water and vanilla extract.

On high heat stir to boiling. Reduce heat to medium. Continue to stir and cook until cranberries pop and mixture has the consistency of jam (*about 2 minutes*).

Remove from heat. Set aside.

In a medium-sized bowl combine oats, brown sugar, and flour. Using a pastry cutter, cut in butter until mixture forms crumbs.

Sprinkle **half** of the oatmeal mixture on the bottom of the greased pan. Spread filling over the oatmeal mixture in pan. Sprinkle remaining oatmeal mixture over filling.

Bake at 350 degrees for about 45 minutes or until top is golden and juice from the berries bubbles through.

Cool on a wire rack for 15 minutes.

Serve warm with your favorite ice cream

Makes 6 servings.

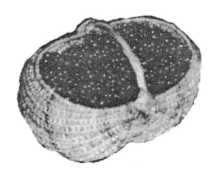

Pies & Puddings

Granny's Freckled Pie

◆ Pastry for a double-crust pie

¾ cup dark-brown sugar, firmly packed
¼ cup all-purpose flour
1 tsp. ground cinnamon
4 Granny Smith apples, peeled, cored, and
      thinly sliced
2 cups fresh cranberries, cut in half
1 Tbsp. butter

Preheat oven to 425 degrees.

Pastry-line a 9-inch glass pie plate.

In a large bowl combine brown sugar, flour, and cinnamon.

Add apples and cranberries. Toss gently until fruits are covered.

Pour mixture into the lined pie plate.

Dot with butter.

Place top crust over fruit filling. Seal and flute the edge. Cut slits in the top crust.

Bake at 425 degrees for about 35 to 40 minutes (cover edge of crust with strips of foil after the first 10 to 15 minutes of baking) or until top is golden brown.

Cool completely on a wire rack.

Makes 8 servings.

Mile-High Bumbleberry Pie

◆ Pastry for a double-crust pie

¾ cup sugar
2 Tbsp. cornstarch
1 tsp. ground cinnamon
5 medium baking apples, peeled, cored, and
    thinly sliced
1 cup fresh cranberries, cut in half
1 cup blueberries, fresh or frozen
1 Tbsp. butter

Preheat oven to 425 degrees.

Pastry-line a 9-inch glass pie plate.

In a large bowl combine sugar, cornstarch, and cinnamon.

Add apples, cranberries, and blueberries. Toss gently until fruits are covered.

Pour mixture into the lined pie plate.

Dot with butter.

Place top crust over fruit filling. Seal and flute the edge. Cut slits in the top crust.

Bake at 425 degrees for about 35 to 40 minutes (cover edge of crust with strips of foil after the first 10 to 15 minutes of baking) or until top is golden. Juice from the fruits will start to bubble over the crust.

Cool completely on a wire rack.

Makes 8 servings.

Nana's Nantucket Cranberry Pie

Laurie Logan graciously shared her favorite cranberry pie recipe with me, which belongs to her grandmother, Norma DiCarlo, who lives in Lakeville with her husband Joseph on the same farm where she was born and grew up.

"My Nana received many cranberry recipes, including this one, from friends and acquaintances when her son worked the bogs in Nantucket. In order to distinguish this pie from her other popular pies she started calling it Nantucket Cranberry Pie."

The DiCarlos and their children have been in the cranberry business for twenty-five years. Their granddaughter Laurie and her husband also own a cranberry bog that produces enough cranberries for their own use and to share with family and friends. During harvest season Laurie, owner of Laurie's Country Cutting, always has fresh cranberries available for her customers (who have become her friends over the years) to take home. Not only do they go home with a top-notch haircut but also some local cranberries to create their own special recipe.

Cranberry Mixture
2 cups fresh cranberries
½ cup sugar
⅓ cup chopped walnuts

Batter
2 large eggs
1 cup sugar
1 cup all-purpose flour
¾ cup (1½ sticks) butter, melted **and cooled**

Preheat oven to 325 degrees.

Grease well a 10-inch glass pie plate with butter. (Nana uses Crisco®.)

Spread dry, whole cranberries evenly on the bottom of the pie plate.

Sprinkle sugar and chopped walnuts over the cranberries. Set aside.

In a large bowl beat eggs well until foamy. Gradually add sugar, beating after each addition, until mixture is thick and light.

In a medium-sized bowl combine flour and cooled, melted butter. Add this mixture to the egg mixture and beat until well blended.

Pour batter over the top of the cranberry mixture.

Bake at 325 degrees for 50 minutes.

Cool on a wire rack.

Makes 8 servings.

Blushing Betty

According to The American Heritage Dictionary of the English Language *a "brown Betty" is "a baked pudding of chopped or sliced apples, bread crumbs, raisins, sugar, butter, and spices". A great lover of cranberries I combined my two favorites — fresh and sweetened dried cranberries — to create this recipe. I hope you enjoy this Blushing Betty as much as I enjoyed creating it for everyone to enjoy, especially my husband, who must give his smile of approval before a recipe goes to print.*

2 cups cranberries, fresh or frozen
1 cup water
¾ cup sugar
½ tsp. ground cinnamon
2 cups soft wheat bread, toasted, cut into one-
half-inch cubes
½ cup sweetened dried cranberries
1 large Granny Smith apple, peeled, cored, and
thinly sliced
2 Tbsp. (¼ stick) butter

Preheat oven to 375 degrees.

Generously butter the bottom and sides of a 9-inch square baking pan.

In a small saucepan combine cranberries, water, sugar, and cinnamon. On high heat stir to boiling.

Reduce heat to medium-high. Continue to stir and cook until cranberries pop and mixture begins to thicken (*about 7 minutes*). Set aside.

To assemble the Betty in layers:
Line the bottom of the baking pan with **half** of the bread cubes. Sprinkle **half** of the sweetened dried cranberries and arrange **half** of the sliced apples evenly. Then spoon **half** of the cooked cranberries over the apples; dot with **one tablespoon** of butter.

Place the remaining bread cubes on top, sprinkle the remaining sweetened dried cranberries, and arrange the remaining sliced apples evenly.

Finish by spooning the remaining cooked cranberries over the apples and dotting the top with the remaining tablespoon of butter.

Cover with aluminum foil and bake at 375 degrees for about 40 minutes or apples are soft and juice from the fruits begins to bubble.

Serve warm with whipped cream.

Makes 6 to 8 servings.

Crusty Cranberry Pudding

This recipe is for those who like their sweets on the tart side. Biting into each whole berry releases a pleasing burst of tartness.

2½ cups cranberries, fresh or frozen
½ cup dark-brown sugar
½ cup chopped walnuts
1 large egg
¼ cup granulated sugar
½ cup all-purpose flour
⅓ cup butter, melted

Preheat oven to 425 degrees.

Grease well a 10-inch glass pie plate with butter.

Spread cranberries evenly on the bottom of the pie plate.

Sprinkle brown sugar and chopped walnuts over the cranberries. Set aside.

In a large bowl beat egg until foamy. Gradually add sugar, beating after each addition, until mixture is thick and light.

Add flour and melted butter. Beat until well blended.

Pour batter over cranberry and nut mixture.

Bake at 425 degrees for 20 to 25 minutes until top is golden brown and juice from berries bubbles through.

Serve warm with your favorite ice cream.

Makes 6 servings.

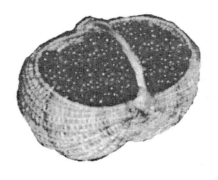

Cookies & Sweets

Robin's Cranberry Softie Cookies

This unique cookie recipe was given to me by a talented Lakeville photographer who not only enjoys cooking but also has a keen eye for nature. Robin sells her nature photographs along with her needle felting and wood carvings at fairs and festivals throughout southeastern Massachusetts.

¼ cup (½ stick) butter, softened
¾ cup dark-brown sugar
1 large egg
1 tsp. vanilla extract
1½ cups all-purpose flour
½ tsp. baking soda
¾ cup fresh cranberries, cut in half
½ cup chopped walnuts (optional)

Preheat oven to 375 degrees.

In a large bowl beat butter, brown sugar, egg, and vanilla extract until light and fluffy.

Add flour and baking soda. Mix on low speed until combined.

Fold in cranberries and chopped walnuts.

Drop dough by rounded teaspoonfuls 2 inches apart onto ungreased cookie sheet.

Bake at 375 degrees for 10 to 12 minutes.

Makes about 30 cookies.

Cranberry Oatmeal Cookies

1 cup rolled oats
1 cup all-purpose flour
½ cup sugar
½ tsp. baking powder
½ tsp. baking soda
½ tsp. ground cinnamon
1 large egg, beaten with a fork
⅓ cup butter, melted
1 tsp. vanilla extract
½ cup sweetened dried cranberries

Preheat oven to 375 degrees.

In a large bowl combine oats, flour, sugar, baking powder, baking soda, and cinnamon.

Add beaten egg, melted butter, and vanilla extract. Mix well with a spoon.

Fold in sweetened dried cranberries.

Drop dough by rounded teaspoonfuls 2 inches apart onto ungreased cookie sheet.

Bake at 375 degrees for 10 to 12 minutes or until cookies are golden brown.

Cool cookies on a wire rack.

Makes 24 cookies.

Cranberry Macaroons

⅓ cup butter, softened
¾ cup sugar
1 large egg
1 tsp. vanilla extract
1 cup all-purpose flour
¾ cup sweetened flaked coconut
½ cup fresh cranberries, cut in half

Preheat oven to 375 degrees.

In a large bowl beat butter, sugar, egg, and vanilla extract until light and fluffy.

Add flour. Mix on low speed until combined.

Fold in coconut and cranberries.

Drop dough by rounded teaspoonfuls 2 inches apart onto ungreased cookie sheet.

Bake at 375 degrees for 10 to 12 minutes or until golden brown around the edges.

Makes 24 cookies.

Cranberry Cocoa Bites

¼ cup unsweetened cocoa powder
⅓ cup warm water
¼ cup extra-virgin olive oil
⅓ cup granulated sugar
¼ cup dark-brown sugar, firmly packed
2 large egg whites, beaten with a fork
1 tsp. vanilla extract
¾ cup all-purpose flour
½ tsp. baking powder
¼ tsp. salt
⅓ cup sweetened dried cranberries

Preheat oven to 350 degrees.

Lightly grease an 8-inch square baking pan.

In a large bowl stir cocoa powder and warm water until smooth. Let stand for 5 minutes.

Add olive oil, sugars, egg whites, and vanilla extract. Stir with a spoon until combined and smooth. Use the back of the spoon to break down any lumps.

In a small bowl combine flour, baking powder, and salt. Add to the large bowl. Mix with a spoon until the dry ingredients are moistened.

Fold in sweetened dried cranberries.

Pour batter into greased baking pan.

Bake at 350 degrees for 20 to 25 minutes or until toothpick inserted in center comes out clean.

Cool completely on a wire rack before cutting.

Makes 16 bites.

Speckled Hermits

3 cups all-purpose flour
1 cup sugar
1 tsp. baking soda
1 tsp. ground cinnamon
½ tsp. ground nutmeg
½ tsp. salt
½ cup extra-virgin olive oil
½ cup skim milk
½ cup molasses
¾ cup sweetened dried cranberries

Preheat oven to 350 degrees.

Grease a 13- x 9- x 2-inch baking pan.

In a large bowl combine flour, sugar, baking soda, cinnamon, nutmeg, and salt.

Add olive oil, milk, and molasses. Mix with a spoon until the dry ingredients are moistened and batter forms a ball.

Fold in sweetened dried cranberries.

Pour batter into greased pan. Using a spatula spread batter evenly into the corners.

Bake at 350 degrees for 25 minutes or until tooth-pick inserted in center comes out clean.

Cool completely on a wire rack before cutting.

Makes 24 hermits.

Cranberry Walnut Pizza

◆ Pastry for a single-crust pie

2 cups fresh cranberries, cut in half
½ cup chopped walnuts
¼ cup sugar
1 Tbsp. dark-brown sugar
½ Tbsp. cornstarch

   Confectioners' sugar, sifted
      (to sprinkle over top after baking)

Preheat oven to 400 degrees.

Line a 14-inch pizza pan with aluminum foil.

Roll pie crust on a lightly floured board into a 13-inch circle. Place dough on the lined pizza pan. Set aside.

In a large bowl combine cranberries, chopped walnuts, sugars, and cornstarch. Pour mixture into the center of the pie crust. Using a spatula spread cranberry mixture evenly over crust leaving a 2-inch border around the outer edge.

Fold crust over cranberries, pinching as needed, to keep filling in place.

Bake at 400 degrees for 20 to 25 minutes or until crust is golden brown and juice from the berries starts to bubble over the crust.

Cool on a wire rack for about 10 minutes.

Serve warm with a light sprinkle of confectioners' sugar.

Makes 6 servings.

About the Photographer

Sandra Denton became interested in photography at an early age. She won her first awards from the Photography Club at Whitman High School. After graduation in 1955 she pursued her passion for photography, becoming a member of the Greater Brockton Camera Club and later serving as judge and commentator. Over the years her expertise has spread to all facets of photography, including portraits. She is best known for her outstanding work in nature photography, a category for which she has won many awards. It's no wonder! Sandra spends all her available time with her backpacking camera gear, either walking through woods looking for a hidden waterfall to photograph, or cruising on a boat seeking pictures of yet another lighthouse to add to her collection.

Her photographs are exhibited in many places throughout the area, such as Stonehill College, Bridgewater Library, and Rockland Trust Company, to name a few. She continues to win numerous awards from the Taunton Art Association and New England Wildlife Art Exposition. Besides nature photography, Sandra enjoys bird carving.

She lives in Bridgewater, Massachusetts.

About the Author

Yolanda Lodi loves to create nutritious and easy to prepare dishes to satisfy her taste and to share with family and friends. She is the author of three previous cookbooks: *Yolanda's Cranberry Country Recipes*, an eclectic collection of traditional and original recipes; *Yolanda's Hand-Me-Down Recipes*, an assortment of recipes rich in New England's cultural heritage; and *Yolanda's Blueberry Cookbook,* so far her most popular cookbook, not only in Massachusetts but also in Maine. Compiling these collections brought so much enjoyment to her that she decided to compile an *All New Cranberry Cookbook*, with recipes that use not only fresh and frozen cranberries but sweetened dried cranberries as well. Besides recipes and stories, this new cookbook features an introduction in which she offers encouragement for those who love to cook and want to be creative in developing their own recipes. "Experiment and take the plunge," she urges her readers. "Try something new that sounds good."

Yolanda looks forward to discussing the process of compiling and preserving recipes with those she meets while promoting her new book. She strongly feels that preserving recipes keeps traditions alive for future generations to cherish.

She lives in southeastern Massachusetts with her husband, Ed, her greatest fan and taste tester.

Notes

Notes

Notes

Notes